Manners

on Holiday

Arianna Candell · Rosa M. Curto

BOOK HOUSE

Hooray, holiday!

Sara

It's summer, and today Peter and Sara are going camping with their Mum and Dad. The sun is shining and it's a beautiful day. Peter is so excited that he is bumping into everything as he rushes around looking for things to take with him. His sister laughs as she watches him. She tells him to calm down before he breaks something or hurts himself!

Peter

4

Fasten your seat belt

The kids jump into the car and fasten their seat belts. Peter feels something sticky on his hand. Yuk! It's a gooey old toffee. When Sara sees it, she remembers that she dropped a toffee the other day! She forgot to pick it up. Now they can see why Mum and Dad don't like them eating in the car.

Peter

Lunchtime

Sara and Peter are glad that Mum and Dad have decided to stop for a picnic lunch. They're tired of being stuck in the car, even though they have been singing and playing games. Sara is so hungry that she gobbles her food and forgets to close her mouth when she eats. She's making a mess of the table and forgets to use her napkin to wipe her mouth. Mum and Dad are frowning so Peter reminds her about her table manners.

Sara

Good afternoon!

They finally arrive at the lake. Sara and Peter soon meet other people and Sara asks them all sorts of questions about bats. She loves bats and would really like to see one at night. Peter is bursting with questions, too, but he's too shy to ask. Unlike his sister, Peter has trouble talking to people that he doesn't know.

Peter   Sara

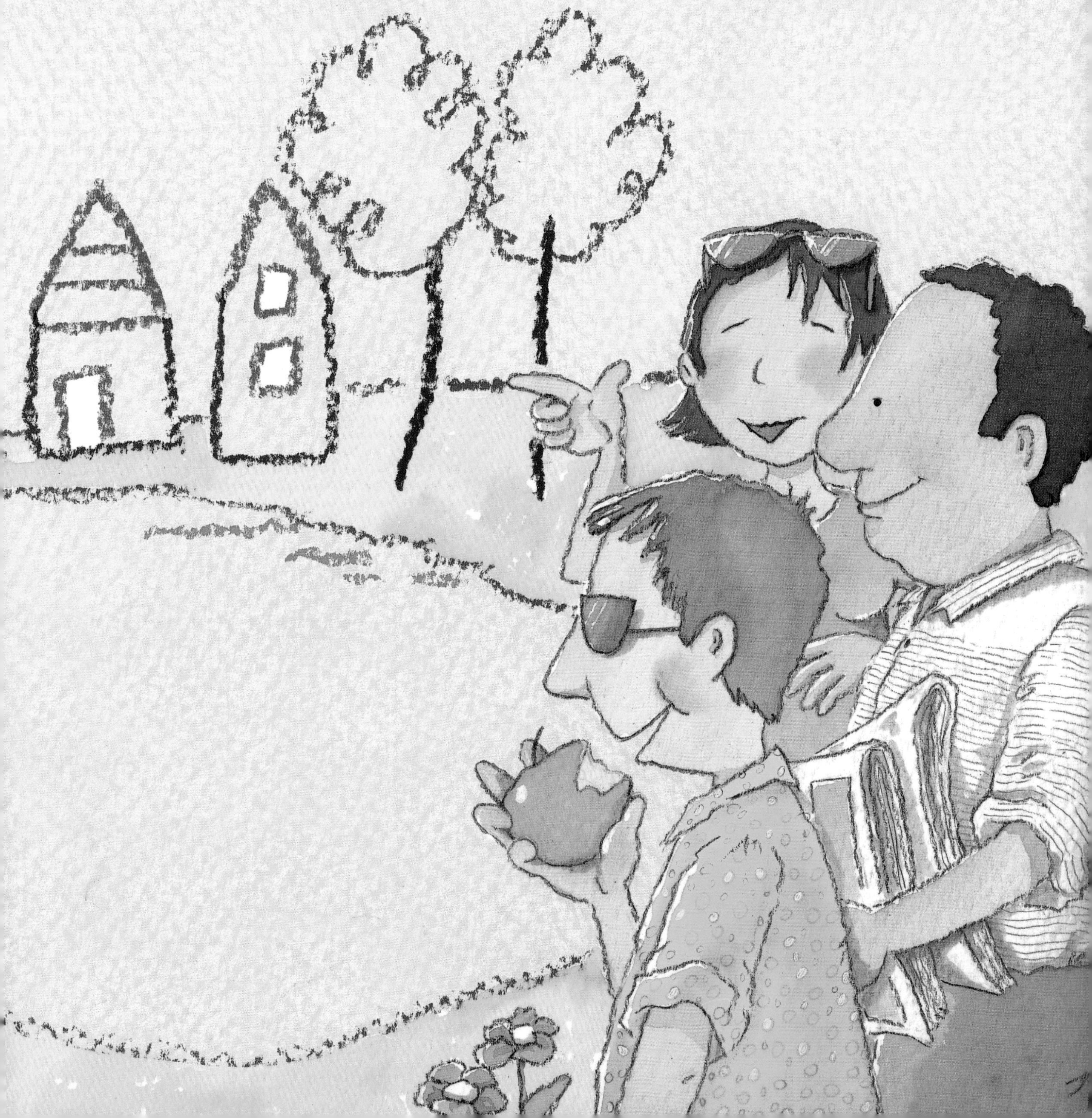

Sara

Peter

Lots and lots of dirt

This place is great! There's lots of grass, sand, rocks, mud and water. There's so much to do and lots of kids to play with. By the end of the day Peter and Sara are filthy: they've got sand in their hair, in their ears, and even in their tummy buttons! Dad cuts Peter's fingernails so they won't get so full of dirt tomorrow and Mum mends the tear in Sara's T-shirt. It's time for the kids to climb into the bath and get clean again.

Sara

Peter

A day trip

Today the children are going on a day trip up
the mountain with their new friends. It's very
hot so they must all wear hats and sun cream
to protect them from the sun. They need
bottles of water to drink, some food and a
small first-aid kit – so everyone carries
something. The youngest boy wants to
take a huge toy truck with him. The others
tell him that he'll get tired carrying it,
and it wouldn't be fair if someone else
had to carry it for him.

Doing chores

Even when they're on holiday, Peter and Sara still have to help with chores. They have to clean the table and set it, empty the bins, make their beds and keep all their own things tidy.

Peter

They hate doing chores, but today Sara really doesn't feel like helping because she has a cold. Peter gives her a tissue for her nose to remind her to keep her germs to herself when she coughs or sneezes!

Sara

Being different

A new family arrived at the lake this morning. Oliver is the same age as Peter, and his brother Harry, is older. Harry can't jump or run very well or catch a ball like other kids can. Oliver says people sometimes laugh at Harry. He explains to them that his brother is just 'different' so that they won't be mean to Harry. Sara says that Harry is the best whistler she's ever heard!

Sara

Jack

Oliver

Peter

Harry

Sophie

At the swimming pool

The kids are having such fun in the pool! They laugh and squeal and splash each other until they accidentally splash a man at the edge of the pool. They apologise to him, but the man is so angry that his face turns as red as a tomato. He does have a right to be cross, doesn't he? Everyone wants to enjoy their holiday.

Home again

Sara and Peter are back home now. Rachel and Maria have sent them a postcard with a lovely view of the beach. Maria said her mum scolded her for racing about on the sand and bothering people. She was cross at her mum so she went off to look for shells instead, but she got lost! Luckily, the lifeguard helped her to find her mum and dad again. Wow! That must have been scary!

Rachel

Maria

Peter

Julia

Alfie

Carla

Sara

Silence!

Julia's mum has invited Sara and Peter to a puppet show. As soon as they get there, Julia's little sister says she's thirsty and wants her mum. She never stops talking and just can't sit still, no matter how hard she tries. When the show is over, she claps the loudest. Bravo!

Emily

Rosie

Animals

Peter and Sara love all animals, but they feel sorry to see them in cages at the zoo. They watch the monkeys: one of them is scratching its nose while another one eats a banana. Peter wants to be a vet when he grows up, and he knows that you shouldn't feed the animals or bother them in any way. Zoo animals must be treated properly — they are not like pets.

Peter

Sara

Pillow fight

Parents sometimes like to go out by themselves, to see a film or something, so Sara and Peter are staying with their cousins tonight. They had pizza for supper, and now that it's time for bed they are having a pillow fight! What a mess. They can't find the clock, their slippers, or the baby's teddy bear. It's time to put everything back where it should be before the grown-ups see the mess!

Chloe

Peter

Josh

Rosie

Jim

Mo

Mark

Maria

Peter

Julia

Anna

Back to school

Back at school, it's great seeing all their friends again to share their summer adventures. Rachel and Maria have been to Scotland. Jim stayed at home because his gran was sick, and his mum and dad wanted to take care of her. Mo has learned how to make kites, and Mark helped his parents to paint their house. What do you think you will do in your school holiday?

Lucy

Activities

STAYING OVERNIGHT

Ask your parents if some friends can stay overnight at your house and make some pizzas for supper. Ask your mum to buy pizza bases at the supermarket and to help you prepare the ingredients for the toppings: diced ham, olives, small chunks of sausage... whatever you like best. First you spread tomato purée on each pizza base, then add your toppings. Finally, sprinkle each one with grated cheese. Ask mum to cook the pizzas for you in the oven – and supper is ready. You'll love this pizza!

THE MIRROR

You need at least two players for this game with one as the 'mirror'. Stand facing each other, because the game is about copying the other player's movements. When you move an arm or leg, or make a face, the 'mirror' has to copy every movement as best he can. He should not laugh or move unless you do. After a while, change roles so that you become the 'mirror'.

Maria   Julia

NUTTY SHIPS

You don't need a windy day to sail your own ship! You can make a sailing boat so small that you can sail it in the bath. All you need are some walnuts, small rectangles of coloured paper and some toothpicks.

Carefully break open the walnut, eat the nut, and keep both halves of the shell. Use the toothpick to pierce a tiny hole in the top and bottom edges of the paper sail. Slot the toothpick through one hole and then the other to make a sail. Put a small ball of modelling clay or play dough inside the shell to hold the sail in place. If you make enough ships like this, you will have a fleet of vessels.

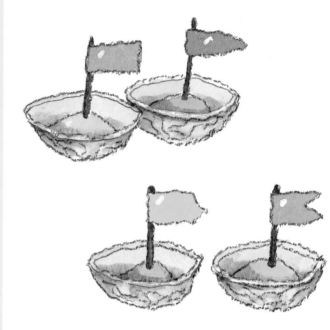

KNOCK DOWN THE TOWER!

You will love this game, you'll see! It's like bowling, only different. You need ten empty cans and different-coloured paper to cover them (optional). Stack the cans up to form a pyramid. Then gather several small balls – tennis balls are ideal. The more kids who play, the more fun you'll have, but you can also play this game by yourself. If you play with others, be sure to take turns throwing the ball and rebuilding the stack. The player who knocks down the most cans with just one throw (or one roll of the ball) is the winner.

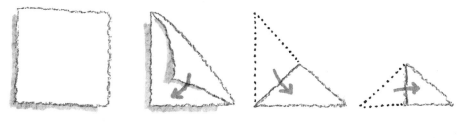

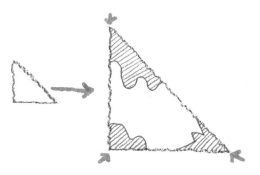

STAINED GLASS WINDOWS

Windowpanes with different colours are very pretty, so this is a way you can make your windows at home look beautiful.

Follow the diagrams (left):

(A) Take a square of black paper (or any dark colour). (B) Fold it diagonally to make a triangle. (C) Fold the triangle in half again. (D) Fold in half again to make a much smaller triangle. (E) Draw different shapes on each corner and cut them out. (F) Unfold the paper and you will see the pattern you have created. Glue coloured tissue paper or cellophane to the back of the sheet of paper and tape it to a windowpane. You will have a window that looks like stained glass.

 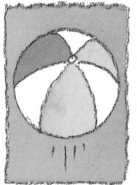 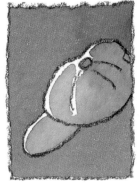  

Guidelines for parents

RESPONSIBILITIES

There is no point making a long list of the things you would like your child to do. It will be easier for both of you if you put him or her in charge of small tasks. For example, your child can be responsible for asking you to cut his nails when there is dirt under them that he can't get out. He can tell you if he breaks something, gets dirty, or if a button falls off his shirt. Don't just scold him for accidents. Instead, ask him how it happened, and calmly let him know how you feel about it. It's important for your child to start feeling responsible for his own belongings and personal hygiene within appropriate age expectations. He can gradually begin to help at home, doing small chores such as putting his dirty clothes in the washing basket, putting shoes away, picking up toys and, when he is a little older, folding his clothes. To make chores easier, show him where things go and make these places easily accessible to him. When children help, it often means more work for you! Remember that the effort really is worthwhile as you are helping your child to become an independent individual.

HABITS

Day-to-day habits are learned more easily and become automatic for children when there is some routine involved: eating at the same time every day, cleaning the table after meals, washing hands, brushing teeth, and so forth. However, if you don't like the regimentation of routine, you might choose other aids for your child. You could use drawings as a reminder. Some suggestions could be: stick a drawing of a toothbrush on the bathroom mirror, or a picture of a laundry basket with dirty clothes around it, or a photo of a 'lonely' shoe without its partner. It's often more effective to use

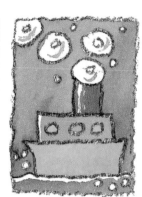

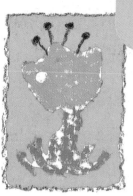

humour than to argue and shout. When your child can read, you might use short prompts like sticking a note inside the front door saying, 'Got your sandwich?' This should eventually teach him to put his lunch in his backpack without reminders. Try not to be repetitive or bullying since your child may begin to tune out and resent your nagging.

WE ARE ALL DIFFERENT

On pages 16 and 17 we meet Harry, a child who is not able to do as many things as his younger brother. This is a good time to explain disabilities and differences to your child. She may already have encountered people who cannot see well or those confined to wheelchairs. She may also have come across people with emotional difficulties who seem to be inappropriately bad-tempered. Ask her to imagine how she might feel if she had to face these difficulties. It is so important for children to begin to understand that we all have our strengths and weaknesses physically, intellectually, and even emotionally. We must find our own strengths but also recognise the talents of others whether they are good at listening, understanding, swimming, drawing or even whistling really well!

SPACES FOR FREEDOM

Young children should be allowed the space to be free from constant adult judgement and scrutiny. If safety is a concern with the very young, their activities can be monitored surreptitiously. Now and then, they should be able to get dirty and not feel guilty if they get their shoes muddy or their clothes torn. While hygiene is fundamental, it is also necessary that children learn to take responsibility for themselves. Part of growing up involves taking moderate risks without constant adult supervision and scolding. Children who are overprotected and not allowed to make decisions can become either insecure or rebellious. It's also important that children understand that there's a time and place for everything. They can have fun and freedom but must not disturb others as they play. If children are exposed to different kinds of environments, they can learn to adapt their behaviour accordingly.

Published in Great Britain in MMXII by
Book House, an imprint of
The Salariya Book Company Ltd
25 Marlborough Place, Brighton BN1 1UB
www.salariya.com
www.book-house.co.uk

1 3 5 7 9 8 6 4 2

A CIP catalogue record for this book is available
from the British Library.

Printed and bound in China.

PB ISBN: 978-1-908177-13-1

Original title of the book in Catalan: Com ens hem de comportar durant les vacances
© MMV Gemser Publications S.L.

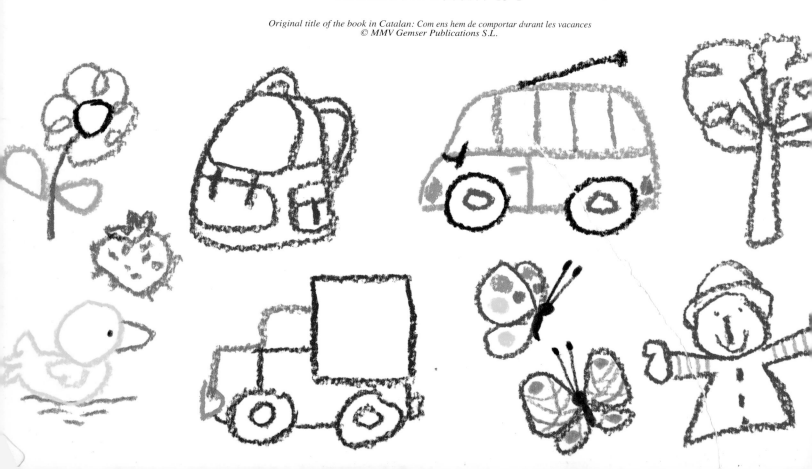